KT-416-378

TALKING DEAD

A Spillage of Mercury
Spanish Fly
Demolition

TALKING DEAD

Neil Rollinson

CAPE POETRY

Published by Jonathan Cape 2015

2 4 6 8 10 9 7 5 3 1

Copyright © Neil Rollinson 2015

Neil Rollinson has asserted his right under the
Copyright, Designs and Patents Act 1988 to be
identified as the author of this work

First published in Great Britain in 2015 by
Jonathan Cape
20 Vauxhall Bridge Road,
London SW1V 2SA

www.vintage-books.co.uk

A Penguin Random House Company

Penguin
Random House
UK

global.penguinrandomhouse.com

A CIP catalogue record for this book is available from the British Library

ISBN 9780224097291

Penguin Random House is committed to a sustainable future for
our business, our readers and our planet. This book is made from
Forest Stewardship Council® certified paper

MIX
Paper from
responsible sources
FSC® C013056

Typeset in Bembo by Palimpsest Book Production Ltd, Falkirk, Stirlingshire

Printed and bound in Great Britain by TJ International Ltd, Cornwall

Time before and time after

T. S. Eliot

Desire may be dead
and still a man can be
a meeting place for sun and rain,
wonder outwaiting pain
as in a wintry tree.

D. H. Lawrence

for Sam

CONTENTS

TALKING DEAD – THE WALL

It was a day like any other
when they came for us.
This was the world we knew,
except the light was different:
the sky, the leaves, the distant sea.
We held hands as we walked,
and they walked behind us,
smoking cigarettes, talking
in hushed tones, embarrassed.
Only the colours troubled me,
the dandelions, how bright they were.
I hadn't noticed that before.
The world will carry on, you said,
but I wasn't sure. I had an intuition
that once I was gone
it was the end for everyone.
You gripped my hand as we
came to the wall. You were the one
true constant in everything.
The stone was warm, we could feel
the heat against our backs.
There was a scent of marjoram.
The sea was blue, and a single ferry
sailed out of the harbour.

ODE TO A MAGNOLIA TREE

magnolia denudata

Impatient
as always,
you blossom
in the cold
March air,
even before
your leaves
have set:
impetuous,
hostage
to late frosts,
the unfinished
business of winter –
but what
do you care,
you want
to cut free,
feel the sun
on your face,
to flaunt
your big
creamy flowers,
so exotic
in this dull
suburban garden.
I see you
in Rio,
on the banks
of the Mississippi,
or holding court
in a Japanese garden.
You glow

2

in the dusk,
your petals
like lanterns,
lighting
the garden wall,
eccentric, ornate
as an art-nouveau
chandelier.
The daffodils
are hesitant,
the crocuses
reluctant to stir.
Only the snowdrops
have come,
and gone,
the ground
hard
as a tin lid.
But look at you:
shivering in the cold,
half-dressed
for a party
that never happened,
standing alone,
unchaperoned
on the cold lawn.
You're not
of this world
really,
so delicate;
stunning
for a week,
and then
the hailstones
ruin you,
the gales,

the sudden
downpours.
The pavements
are strewn
with flotillas
of little ivory
rowing boats
as if some
ocean liner
had just
gone down
with all hands
lost.

CHRISTMAS IN ANDALUCIA

I'm in the bath when you pop up
for a drink between turkey and pudding:
you with your G & T, me with my vodka and coke.
It is dark there in Surrey, while here
a late sun gleams in the olive groves.
Christmas in Andalucia:
the search for sunshine, the good life,
in a plush hotel – the mini-bar
stuffed with cheese, chorizo and olives,
a bottle of cava on ice. I have the laptop
on a stool at the side of the bath,
and you have yours at the end of your bed.
You look delicious in your new black bra,
far away in that cold stone house.
Beyond the dark window, England
is covered in frost and moonlight.
Soon they're calling you down for pudding,
cheese, and a good sweet wine, for games
around the fire. I ask you to take off your bra
before you go. I am full of loss and longing.
You slip the straps from your shoulders
and let it fall. The miles are meaningless.
You try to escape but can't; the heart
is hewn from elm and oak and mistletoe.

Winter figs,
come to the branches
twisted with cold.

Tough, solid, obstinate,
so different to their soft-headed
summer friends.

They are red inside
like a sunset, icy
without a hint of summer,

wild, suspicious
of every whisper in the leaves.
Between their sour lips

they hold a crease of sugar.
Unexpected visitors,
they leave exactly as they came,

in emptiness and in the dark,
stunned for a moment
by the light.

A country lane, riding home
through a deep frost.
It was like the headlong rush
into sleep. The way it happened:
the calm, balletic movement
of my bike through the air.
The world was spinning.
When I came to rest,
I could feel the cold moss
against my cheeks. I was high
above everything.
I could see the driver of the car
stare through the windscreen,
my torso laid on the road,
steaming in the headlights.
It was difficult to think.
I remember the beauty
of the solid world, the lights
of a distant city, stars in the sky,
all of it fading fast.
I thought: if I don't call now,
they'll never find my head up here.
I tried to shout but I didn't know how.
A blackbird was singing in my ear.

PICNIC

How different it is under the sky,
   on your knees, steadying her hips
      as you ride her, that sweet nut

of pleasure in the perineum.
   You like it like this, out in the open,
      wilder, more atavistic, your head

dizzy as you scan the fields,
   the hedgerows; vulnerable now
      to predators, perverts, coppers.

Miles away a storm is brewing,
   you feel the buzz in your skin, the tickle
      of flies as they land and lift.

She moans as you slap her arse,
   you grunt as her muscles milk you,
      and you move up the hillside,

a creature with six legs – prehistoric
   hominids engaged in battle,
      greased and mucky, plastered with grass

and twigs, fucking like bunnies, rutting
   like deer in England's field, the stag
      and the doe. The birds are singing,

the living are eating the dead, you're rooted,
   conjoined, at one with nature.
      Amazing how good it feels

with the sun on your back, how willing she is,
    how eager you are,
        the whole hill moving, seething

with life, everything feeding
    on everything else, voracious and full
        of appetite. You finish off quickly

and slump on the tartan picnic rug,
    gasping like fish, your genitals wet and itching.
        You roll on your belly and watch the world

as if it were newly minted, her knickers
    laid in the grass like a serviette, your trouser leg
        covered in hummus. Ants are carrying off

pieces of cake as big as their heads;
    bread crumbs, cheese; and a wasp
        lies drunk in a tumbler of wine.

You can hear the storm now, cracking like sheets
    on a clothes line, your skin is electric,
        the hair on your chest is standing on end.

ODE TO A PISS

That throbbing,
dead centre
of the sacrum
where
the kundalini sleeps,
between
the penis
and the sphincter,
like the ache
of love,
or longing.
You've had
a skinful
in the buffet car
and the only toilet
is out of order.
You feel
the pressure
build
as your bladder
swells.
You clench
your buttocks,
you sit cross-legged
and watch
the empty fields
flash by,
the darkening
woods
and rivers,
you count
the stations
one by one,
until,

at last,
you're out
on the platform
mincing
your way
to a fence,
a church wall,
the back entrance
to Sainsbury's.
It gushes
out of you,
frothing
against the stone,
in full view
of the CCTV.
You can smell
the yeast and hops,
the meadows
of England
filling your head.
You lift your face
like a penitent
to the night sky,
the teeming stars.
It feels
like the human soul
has returned
to your body.

THE BIBLE

Big as a suitcase, heavy
as a log, the cover wrinkled
in elephant skin.
Budby opened the book,
and the frontispiece lit up the room;
there were angels and saints,
all the shimmering animals
of heaven. Christ on his cross.
Budby's eyes glimmered
in this new light. What he saw
I do not know, but he grabbed
a corner, as if it were no more
than a photo of Billy Bremner,
and tore the whole page out.
I couldn't believe it.
He folded it up, and stuffed it
in the pocket of his Sunday best.
I can still remember the rip
of the paper, the dust motes
floating in the air of that miserable
Methodist chapel, and I felt
something lift me, like wings,
out of that dark place.

MONSOON

The roads are thigh-deep in sewage.
I wade home, the rain is falling
in huge, voluptuous drops.
It's like a dream: so much water,
but all of it foul, undrinkable.
A white cat, round as a football
bobs in the black water, tampons,
toilet paper, rotten vegetables.
It buckets down all day and night.
I can't sleep for the stench,
the shrieking birds, monkeys
sheltering on the window-ledge.
The couple upstairs are screaming,
the couple downstairs fucking like dogs
in their damp bed – the weariness,
this craving for cold, clean water.
In the morning my black shoes are green
with mould; my throat is on fire.

GANGES

In the early dawn they row.
Two men with a bundle of rags.
The sound of oar-locks
echoes off the palace walls.
There are no women with them,
no mother, no sister.
It is so quiet, you can hear
the splash as they drop the child.
Few can be laid here:
holy men, children and those
who have died by snakebite;
their bones rock in the dark swell
while sufis bathe in the waters.
River dolphins breach
the surface with barely a ripple,
oiled and silvered,
fat on the fertile Ganges.

MOTHER-DIE

Cow Parsley – Anthriscus sylvestris

Those lacy umbrels
swaying in the sun
seemed innocent enough.
I was scared: *mother*
and *die*. What could it mean?
What secret power
did the hedgerows hold?
Budby took it back
to his step-mum's,
hid it in her pillow slip.
We waited all week
but she didn't die.
We fed potato peelings
to the guinea pigs, cremated
spiders in the burning heat
of the magnifying glass,
drowned beetles in bleach.
When I touched the giant hogweed
I came out in welts and lay
like a leper in my bed.
The world was full of dangers:
laburnum, hensbane, foxglove,
everywhere the countryside
shimmered with possibility,
but nothing chilled me
like the mother-die.

GERBIL

The school gerbil
had given birth to a brood
of six pink thumbs.
Budby held out his hand
and showed us one.
It looked like a miniature horse
asleep on his palm,
hairless, all skin and bone.
I just picked it up, he said,
and it broke, like an egg.
I thought he was going to cry,
then he dropped it
in the waste-paper bin
and walked away,
wiping his hand
on the back of his shorts.

NOOBS

We were spawned into mayhem, dumb with fear.
This was all we'd dreamed about, and more.
We saw the smokestacks rising, vapour trails
crossing the sky. We heard the distant boom
of ordnance, and trembled at the prospect.
We stood with our guns: awkward, all fingers
and thumbs – easy pickings.
We learned the landscape quickly,
every nook and cranny, swamp and sniper point.
We heard the wind whistle in the Slipgate Complex.
We saw the bloodbaths of DM4, the places
where we'd die: Chambers of Torment,
the Longest Yard. The slaughter was thrilling,
we were hooked on blood lust; the buzz of a head-shot,
on walking among the dead. We'd fight all night,
and as the dawn came up – when all we could see,
if we closed our eyes, were the butchered *grunts*,
when all we could hear were the screams –
we'd flick the switch to bring us back: the beer cans,
ashtrays piled high, neighbours heading to work,
and we'd sleep at last, through the daylight hours.

THE VERY SMALL BASELINE GROUP
CONVENES AT THE CAT AND FIDDLE

A groaning table of empties makes up
our Very Small Array: a barley-scented
interferometer. Here we can study the cosmos
and drink. We tune in to the microwave sky:
to the froth at the edge of the universe.
We sup in the dusk: everything glows
with its own light, the hedgerows, lawn,
the mass of atoms spinning inside the glass
where the Milky Way sings in a half inch of Guinness;
a song of the distant past when the world
was a moment old. We gather it all in our mugs,
in a pub garden on the edge of the moors
looking down on Jodrell Bank: grand-daddy
of the red-light district, cocking its huge lug
to the whiplash of cosmic strings, to the mayhem
beyond our patch. The bats are in on it,
hunting in ultrasound, catching moths,
while frogs call in the meadows, one to the other,
a vast, unfathomable love-song. I finish my pint
and add my glass to the phalanx: the more we drink
the clearer we see, as any old soak will tell you.
I tip back my head to look at the Pleiades
and tumble, arse over tit, into the damp grass.
I lie in my cups under the bling of the northern sky.
I can hear it call, I can see it clearly now:
all and nothing, the whole sky blazing.

TALKING DEAD – THE OFFICE

The days are timeless here,
we mind our business,
share cigarettes, talk about the past.
We have our work to do.

I sit at my desk and keep an eye
on admissions. I mark them in
and I mark them out. The ledgers
stretch for miles and miles.

We get all sorts through here.
Some stay for the briefest of moments
then disappear. Others seem
reluctant to leave. You find them
wandering from room to room,
inquisitive, happy in their skin.

You can tell who'll be staying,
and who'll be heading back
by the shadows they cast,
the weight of their footfalls.

I stopped a guy last week,
bug-eyed, dazed; he was
off his head with fear,
staring at the light beyond the door,
he had a wife and kids he said,
he really should be getting back.

And, yes there's a corridor, with light
at the end, but it's not the portal
to paradise, it's just a door
to the garden, the orchard,
the hills beyond.

EVENING IN AXARQUÍA

for Richard Skinner

This is as close as you get
to the end of the continent.
Beyond the last mountain
a glimmer of sea turns purple.
There's nothing here but cactus
and bitter almonds. The nuts
crack as they cool, and dogs
are barking from every hill.
I drink a beer at the window,
feeling far from home.
A flock of blue-throats
fly down the valley, chirruping,
heading home to Africa;
you can just see, in the distance,
the coast of Morocco,
the Atlas Mountains as they fade.
This is the loneliest place
on the planet tonight: alien, harsh.
It darkens quickly, and everything falls
into silence – except the dogs,
the indefatigable dogs, barking
mad with the heat and emptiness.

It doesn't hurt a bit, in fact
I felt ecstatic. I could see the bullet,
bright as a star. I could trace
its parabola over the field,
like fishing wire, a pencil line
drawn on paper.

I was, for a moment, a visionary.
I stilled the mayhem, the wind, the rain.
The bullet flew right through my head.
I went down like a sack of spuds.

I saw each of my friends
come and look at me.
Some were frightened
and some were full of sadness.
One held my face and kissed me.

I was far away. I thought of no one.
I was the only living thing in the universe,
and giddy with it all, godlike.
I'd do it again, and again. Yes.
Shoot me again. Oh, shoot me again.

CUCKOO PINT

They have eaten so much of wake robin, that they cannot sleep for love.
John Lyly, *Love's Metamorphosis,* 1601

i Spring

Adam and Eve. Lords and Ladies,
always a thrill finding it among the garlic
and dandelions, that purple stamen
poking from its lacquered hood.
Touch it, if you dare, we'd taunt the girls,
knowing nothing yet of the secret
lore of love and sex – the sap rising
in all of us, our underpants damp,
a root-ache in our balls. The air
was full of pollen, it fell from the trees,
and blew through the grass, we were
sneezing like clowns, wiping snot
on the backs of our hands, innocents agog
in a fecund land. Birds were nesting,
ponds were full of frogspawn,
the woods were set with honey traps,
but Sandra was seventeen, she knew
a thing or two already. We watched
wide eyed as she grabbed the stalk,
and pulled it clean out.

ii Autumn

It throbs
like a poker
in the russet gloom,
the sore
and blistered head
covered
in orange pimples.
This is what comes
of frolicking
in the grass.
It festers
in the leaf mold,
comical,
embarrassing,
beyond help.

THE STORM

(Coleshill 2013)

for Fiona

I watched it move
through yellow fields;
mercurial and sly,
the dark and brooding
cloudshapes flashing
intermittently, grumbling
as it came up the vale.

The trees grew still.
I counted the miles
between us.
It seemed so far away –

and then,
as if someone had lobbed
a stun-grenade
over the fence,

I saw the incandescent heart
of matter, the Technicolor
hedges, dazzled
with rain and lightning.

The house shook,
the fuses blew,
and the windows hummed
like drum skins.

Dusha squealed
and flew into the house,

the cats, hard-wired
for violence,
wandered through
the flower beds
with bloodied mouths,
nonchalant as ever.

And then it was over,
the rain stopped,
the earth drank,
and the lawn steamed in the sun:
all of it tut-tutting.

I went beneath the stairs
to coax the house
out of its funk – the lights
came on, and the fridge
shuddered back to life.

Beyond the garden,
the storm rolled on
towards Oxford,
through wheat fields,
parched and tinder-dry,

and the light, filtered
through thirty thousand feet
of shifting nimbus
lit the landscape like a Constable.

Sparrows squabbled
in the greengage, a collared dove
cooed in the ash, and the radio
resumed its calming commentary
on the cricket.

CHESED SHEL EMET

Every piece of the man shall be gathered:
the scattered spleen, the blue intestines
laid in the Bethlehem sun, bone fragments
peppering the bark of the lemon trees,
the ruined heart, toe-nails, the soft ribbons
of flesh stuck to the synagogue wall.

Some things will never be found:
the blood that ran down the gutter,
the fine mist of viscera that blew
through the shell of the bus; bile
and vitreous, the smoke
that drifted away on a breeze.

FEATHERS

A cold winter's evening between trains;
a man laid out on the cold stone,
two figures knelt over him, in prayer,
a defibrillator laid at his side like a bible.
It speaks to those who want to listen:
this is the end of life, it says, gather round
and watch. An automated voice tells us all
to *stand back, stand back*. It beeps,
then bang! The shock goes through him,
shaking his boots, blowing the down from his coat.
He sleeps on. They give him another shot,
so strong he almost sits up, but settles again
on the platform edge, so tired he will not wake.
The crowd are fascinated. It's been a long day,
but we stay to watch, in the hope he'll rise,
full of electricity, his hair standing on end,
but none the worse for that. They try again.
His body quakes beneath the current,
feathers pour out of him, like light.
You can see the resignation on the faces
of the medics, their body language;
they whisper to each other through the blizzard,
lay the box on his chest and carry him off
through all the mute witnesses: platform two,
Clapham Junction, the air is full of feathers
swirling in the dark like snow.

IN THE LRB BOOKSHOP

He comes shuffling up as I browse
the poetry shelves: Eddie Linden,
half-cut, and though we've met before
he won't remember me. He looks
me up and down for a moment:
You a poet? he asks, in a tone
somewhere between hope and scorn.
No. I'm not. He shakes his head and says:
You look a right fucking mess.
I thought you must have been a poet.

X-RAY SPECS

You shake the paper, hold it
to the window to still
the shimmering newsprint:

football results, the racing form,
marriages, births and deaths:
which reminds you,

as you take your glasses
from the little hinged tomb
where they rest in velvet,

that once you could read
by the light of the moon, or
under covers in the dying beam

of a bicycle lamp, your radio
faint beneath the pillow: Caroline,
Luxembourg, American Forces,

and once, with nothing more
than the X-Ray Specs
you got from Bazooka Joe's,

you saw through the summer dress
of Joy Watson, the beautiful bones
of her body glowing like radium.

Now as you lay your spectacles
back in their box, their arms folded
in solemn pose, all you see is the yellow

blur at the edges of vision, the world shimmering like the cartoon landscape of Crystal Tipps and Alistair.

I do not speak of the moon in the well.
I speak of the colour of cocoa,
the barest flush of pink.
I don't speak of roses and chocolate,
but of soft animal tissue,
of sweet mucosae, damp and trembling,
the threefold entrance to sweetness:
venus of the dark skin,
and a pitch-black pelt.

In the dark ages they took their time.
They knew about pain
and butchered you slowly, whistling
as they went. It was God's work.

The first few minutes were awesome.
I didn't know I could scream like that;
but nothing lasts forever,
the adrenalin kicks in and you're high

as a kite. The skin comes off
like bark from a tree, the soul rises,
and the body breathes.

The Romans were the real pros:
they'd let you live, but slaughter
your wife and children.
You can only suffer
while the breath runs through you;
any torturer knows that.

The clock struck twelve;
I heard twelve strikes
of a shovel in the earth.
This is it, I thought, it's over,
but the silence answered. No.
Not yet. Sleep on a while.
You will not see the final grain
as it trembles in the hourglass.
There are many hours of sleep
on the old shore yet, before
you wake, one clear morning,
and find your boat, moored
on the other bank.

STINKHORN

Nothing as rank
as the stinkhorn, its dark
and slimy head nodding
on a swollen shaft,
covered in flies, wet
with a pungent discharge.
That looks like your dad's cock,
said Budby unzipping his
Slazenger, pockmarked
with pink bruises.
He stood for a moment
taking guard, then took
the bat to its head.
We heard the splat
as he launched it deep
into the trees, a perfect
cover drive, and we
ground the root back down
with the heels of our new
school shoes.

THE COFFEE VARIATIONS

i

Ristretto,
black as a starless night,
demitasse
of dark matter –
hardly more
than a thimbleful,
so dense
it might fall
through the top
of the kitchen table.

ii

I put my nose
to the rising steam:
wraith-like,
crepuscular –
a sparkling
ribbon
of distant
stars
against the dark
shadow
of your overcoat.

iii

Odour
of charred oak,
toffee,
and sphagnum moss,
creosote
warming
on a fence
in the morning sun.
I set it down
on a roadside table.
It shivers
with every passing car,
like a measure
of crude,
shimmering
with rainbows.

iv

I drop a cube
of sugar
into the cup,
it gives off
an effervescence,
like Alka-Seltzer,
a little ghost
of bitterness –
spirit
of the coffee bean.

v

The one
true cure
for hangover,
indolence
and listlessness.
I say my prayers
at the altar of
The Daily Grind,
taking my pew
beside the Gaggia.
I bow my head
to this black brew:
a double shot
of darkest
Guatemalan;
a single sip
and I feel
the blood
hurtle
through my heart,
the pulse
knocking
at my temple
like an animal,
chained and trying
to escape.

vi

I take this pack
of beans
from the fridge,
it rattles
like a swag bag,
a secret hoard
of shiny
black beetles,
their cast-off
wing-casings
clacking
as I pour them
into my hand-
cranked mill.
They shatter
and crack,
releasing a warm
and dusty odour:
arabica, robusta.
I grind them
to the finest dust,
potent
as gunpowder,
ready now
for my
trusty Bialetti
standing guard
on the hob
like an old knight,
its shiny armour
tarnished,
burnt black

in the heat
of battle –
its long years
of conflict
in the coffee wars.

I opened my mouth to breathe,
like I do in dreams,
and the water flowed into me.
I sank like a stone.
At first I thought it was pain;
it was just the beginning of bliss.
I could feel the buds in my throat
palpitate: the obsolescent gills.
I saw the sand eel and tuna,
the plankton lifting in veils.
I breathed so deep I could taste
the salt and seaweed.
And I saw as I fell, the dark
hull of the ship above me,
its cold shadow. Things glittered
in the gloom like stars in the sky.
I saw dolphins, blue and green.
I was laid on the bed and the fish
came in thousands to pick me clean.
I loved the nights there,
the ultramarine, the moonlight,
the ghostly glow of the jellyfish
shifting like cloud above me.

THE TZARINA

for Joanna Härmä

She walks among the horses in the stable
looking for her stallion. He's back
from stud, and the air is thick with the smell
of semen. She can recognise his scent,
the musk of his sweat and breath.
He stands in the cold air, steaming,
lifts his long head to sniff the air.
He can hear her steps, her thin voice calling,
where have you been, my lovely?
She strokes his flank, the sweaty haunch.
His belly is hot, she feels the sea
of his viscera, the pump of his heart.
He's easily roused after the mare,
his penis unfolds, thick as a man's arm.
She licks her palm and holds him
firm in her fist, she can feel the slick
of oils from the female. You naughty boy.
His balls are swollen, plump and sore.
He whinnies, kicks a hoof on the flagstones.
Tonight her boys will lower him over her,
she will hear the harness creak,
the scaffolding groan, she will feel him buck,
and his eyes will shine, like watery planets
in the black cosmos.

The last days were dreadful,
the only peace came in sleep.
I dreamed of a tree, I remember that,
an ancient oak on the edge
of a weathered cliff, and the roots
were struggling for grip.
The whole body of the tree shook,
its vast canopy of leaves
shimmered in the darkness,
and when the cliff crumbled and fell,
the oak rose up in the air and floated
all by itself across the sea.
When I woke I found myself here,
dozing in the chair, and I knew
I'd passed over. George came in
with a cup of tea. I'd never tasted
anything like it before. This was
what the gods must drink, I thought.
I could have wept. I sat by the window;
it was mild, and out on the lawn
children were playing as always.

FOAL

Where has he come from?
Through what vast emptiness
has he travelled to get to this
cold place, full of light and frost?
He stands on four unsteady legs,
the hot breath billowing
out of him. He glistens in a suit
of viscera, electric-blue and green.
What has he seen, what knowledge
has he brought from the secret
heart of matter, this traveller
who only minutes ago landed
in a field at the end of the lane?
He looks at the meaningless world:
a horse-headed god in an alien land,
he clears his throat and whinnies,
and what he means we cannot know;
it could be the answer to everything,
or maybe it's simply – look, I'm a horse,
the air is sweet, and the grass is good.

STARLING

*A small bird will drop frozen dead from a bough
without ever having felt sorry for itself.*
D. H. Lawrence

It crashed on its first, ill-fated flight,
into this box of empty bottles
and beer cans by the back door.

There's no way home for this one now,
whose mother keeps coming to feed it still,
between the cider and the Holsten Pils.

The fledgeling looks me in the eyes
and hisses like a snake.
There's nothing I can do to save it,

or save its mother's grief, if that's
what she feels, pecking the lawn,
pulling fat worms from the rose-bed.

Beyond the box a tantalising birdsong
fills the air, it cocks its head to listen, flaps
a broken wing, then hides behind a can.

Soon the cats will take it apart in the yard,
its mother close by on a fence-post,
shrieking in futile protest.

Tomorrow, at dawn, she'll sing her song
again, without hope or sadness, from the top
of the apple tree, as she always does.

LOVE SONNET XI

after Pablo Neruda

I hunger for your mouth, your voice, your hair.
I pound the streets without food, starving.
Bread doesn't fill me, the dawn unhinges me,
all day I search for the liquid sound of your feet.

I hunger for your slippery laugh,
for your hands, the colour of a savage harvest,
for the pale stones of your fingernails,
I could eat your skin, that flawless almond.

I could swallow the light that fires your beauty,
the sovereign nose on your arrogant face,
the fleeting shadow of your eyelashes.

I'm prowling the streets, famished, sniffing the dusk,
hunting you down, hunting your hot heart
like a puma in the emptiness of Soho.

They cut the collar off my shirt,
tied my arms to my sides,
and laid me on the bench.
When they closed the *lunette*
around my neck, I shut my eyes.

I could hear a mumbled prayer
somewhere behind me,
and then it began:
they released the *mouton*,
it rattled in the runners,
I could hear the air sing
on the lip of the blade.
It fell so slowly,
I thought of all I had loved.
I said goodbye to the earth,
to the past and future;
and the innocent wood
groaned as it shook.

It lopped off my head
like a coconut.
I felt like a child
falling backwards over a fence.
When the world stopped
spinning, I opened my eyes
and saw the sky
enclosed in the wide O
of the wicker basket.

A man looked in, like a giant
peering down a rabbit hole.
I smiled – he frowned,
and I felt the blood

run down my chin.
He reached inside,
a look of fear in his eyes,
ran his fingers through my hair
then lifted me into the light,
like a new born baby.

The crowd were in raptures,
the tricoteuses cursing me
from behind their knitting needles.
I wanted to laugh,
but all I could do was stare.
Beyond the city, the hills
glowed in the morning sun,
I couldn't take my eyes off them,
and then he dropped me
back in the basket.

ACKNOWLEDGEMENTS

Acknowledgements are due to the editors of the following:

Dark Matter – Poems of Space (Calouste Gulbenkian Foundation), *Feeling the Pressure: Poetry and Science of Climate Change* (The British Council), *Magma*, *Manchester Review*, *Poetry*, *Poetry Review*

The sequence 'Talking Dead' originally appeared as a pamphlet of the same name published by Aussteiger Publications, which was shortlisted for the Michael Marks Pamphlet Competition.

Thanks are due to Society of Authors for an extremely generous and timely grant which kept me going through difficult times.